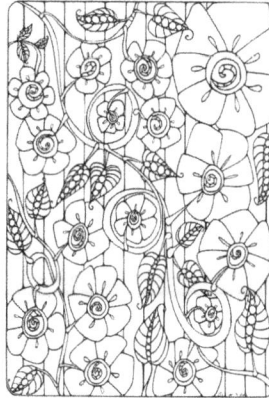

Petal Pusher

a Coloring Book of Flowers
by Patricia Burke

'Petal Pusher'

is published by Coloradoodle Publications

United States of America

Front Cover colored by Shelah Dow

ISBN-13: 978-0-9975959-4-9

ISBN-10: 0997595949

Taylor Ryan,
For your encouragement to finish what I started.
For dropping all those pearls of wisdom about setting my ego aside and accepting critique and criticism without falling apart. For helping me see and believe I could do anything I set my mind to. For showing me that being afraid is okay. For teaching me the fear of "putting yourself out there" could be overcome with tenacity and passion. Your talent and imagination are stunning.
Thank you.

Petal Pusher Coloring Team

Charlotte Schroeder Beeston
Dana LaPorte
Debbie West Commings
Dee Dee Boseman
Elisabeth Anderson
Jennifer Knisley Preston
Jessica Johnson
Kelly Deuber Taylor
Lina Weikel
Marian Radius
Mary 'Diva' Reinecke
Michelle Rood Huntley-Herrema
Rachel Gillham
Shawn Hallenbeck
Shelah Dow

Tech support and video tutorials thankfully accepted from Shelah Dow.

Unwavering friendship, advice and support offered and most gratefully accepted from Shelah, Jess and Kelly...Love you all to bits!

This Book

Belongs to

© 2016 PAB

© 2016 PAB

© 2016 PAB

© 2016 PAC

2017 PAB

© 2010 PAB

© 2016 PAB

© 2017 PAB.

Keep moving forward for your

BONUS PAGES

Happy Coloring!

Find Coloring Books and Pages hand-drawn and Doodled by Patricia Burke at the following websites;

https://www.coloradoodle.com

https://www.gumroad.com/coloradoodle

https://www.facebook.com/coloradoodle

Follow Patricia on;

Instagram @coloradoodle1

**Find Patricia's
Coloring Books
on Amazon.com**

~SHOE-DLES~
http://amzn.to/2ePBHn2

~ZOO-DLES~
http://amzn.to/2gpReYi

~HEARTS~
http://amzn.to/2mEIwc3

For the "print your own books"
downloadable PDF site,
go to...

https://www.gumroad.com/coloradoodle

From the Coloring Book
SHOE-DLES

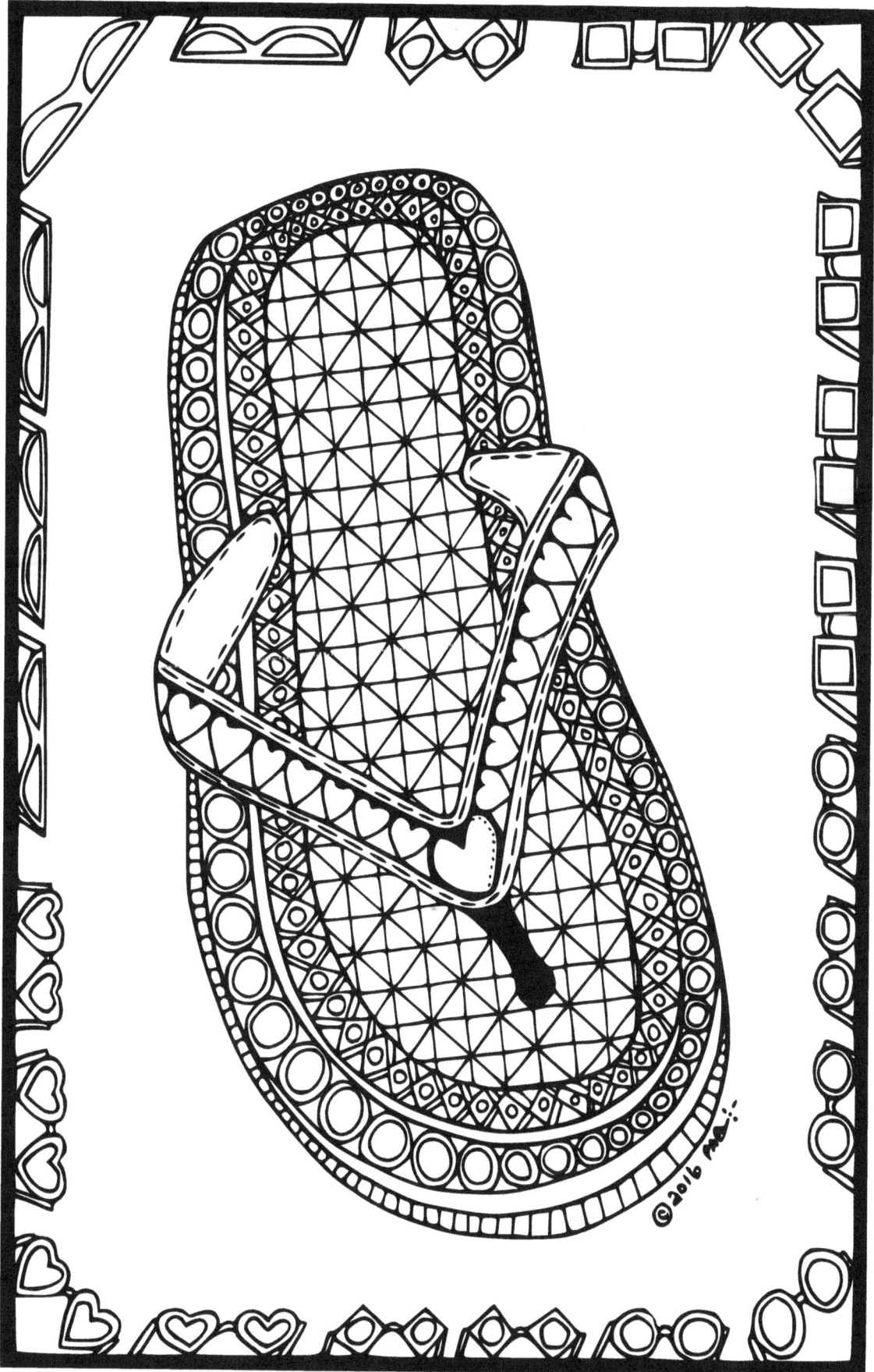

From the Coloring Book, ZOO-DLES

From the Coloring Book, HEARTS,
by Patricia Burke

Blotter Page

Blotter Page

Blotter Page